Fun with Abby & Alyssa ™

An Introduction to Sign Language

A day ends at Bedtime

Written by Grandpa Don ™
Illustrated by Liam Gooley

Dedication

Abby and Alyssa are real people. They both have significant medical challenges and use sign language to talk. As growing sisters, their energy and charisma can be inspirational to anyone that wishes to learn.

This series of books is dedicated to Abby and Alyssa who inspire me, and to Grandma Gina who lives on within our hearts.

Grandpa Don ™

Hi! My name is Abby and this is my sister Alyssa.

Alyssa uses signs instead of words to talk. She makes these signs with her hands.

You already know some signs like waving your hand to say hi.

Come with us and we'll learn more signs!

Hi: Open hand waved side to side.

There are signs for many things, like "sleep".

Let's find other bedtime words and sign them together!

Sleep: Bring the right open hand palm facing left and fingers pointing up, in against the right cheek.

What do we take in a tub?

The Sign: Rub the knuckles of both "10" hands, palms facing in, up and down the side of the chest twice.

That's right, we take a bath in the tub!

Let's all make the sign for bath!

Bath: Rub the knuckles of both "10" hands, palms facing in, up and down the side of the chest twice.

What is the toilet used for?

The Sign: Shake the right "T" hand back and forth with palm facing forward.

Let's all make the sign for potty!

Potty: Shake the right "T" hand back and forth with palm facing forward.

The Sign: Rub right index finger back and forth across front teeth.

That's right, we brush our teeth with toothpaste!

Let's all make the sign for brushing our teeth!

Brush Teeth: Rub right index finger back and forth across front teeth.

What do we wear to bed?

The Sign: Form a "P" and then a "J" with the right hand in front of chest.

That's right, we wear pajamas to bed!

Let's all make the sign for pajamas!

Pajamas: Form a "P" and then a "J" with the right hand in front of chest.

What does Mommy give us before Bedtime?

Arms of both "S" hands crossed at wrist, palms facing in, pull arms back against the chest twice.

Let's all make the sign for hug!

Hug: Arms of both "S" hands crossed at wrist, palms facing in, pull arms back against the chest twice.

The Sign: Hold the right hand open with palm facing forward and touch the middle and ring fingers to palm.

Let's all make the sign for "I love you"!

I love you: Hold the right hand open with palm facing forward and touch the middle and ring fingers to palm.

We've learned
a lot of signs about
Bedtime today.

It's time for
Alyssa and me
to go home...

Let's all make the sign for good-bye!

Good-Bye: Wave open hand up and down.

For more fun with sign language, you can practice your A,B,C's and numbers!

alphabet

A

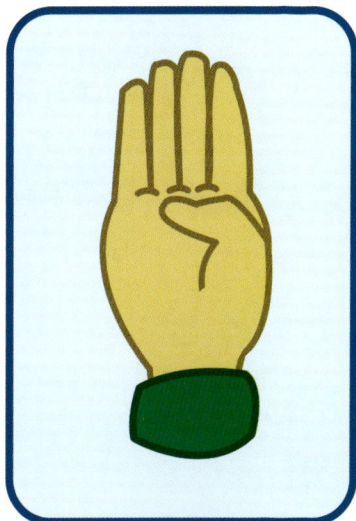

B

C

D

E

F

G

H

I

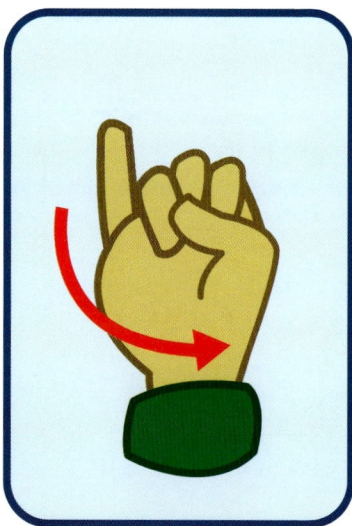

J

K

L

M

N

O

P

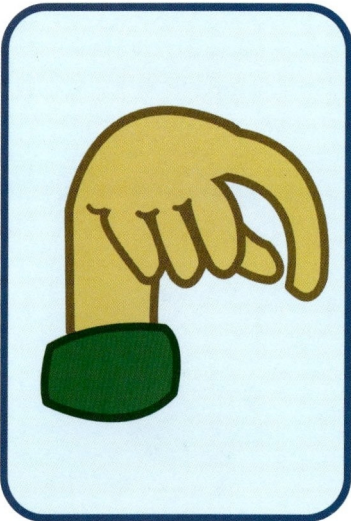

Q

R

S

T

U

V

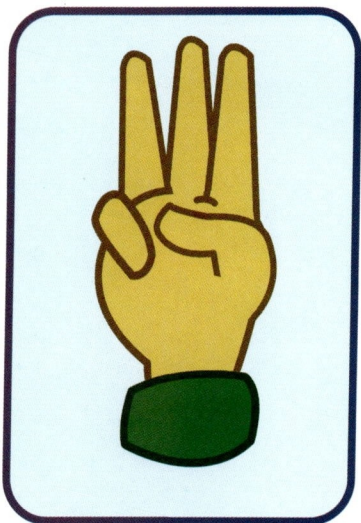

W

X

Y

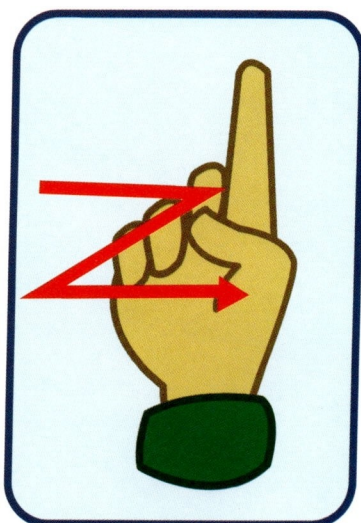

Z

numbers 1 - 10

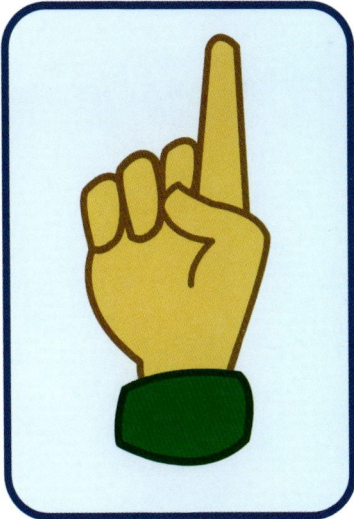

1

2

3

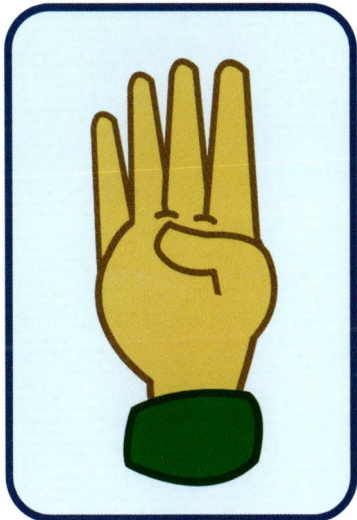

4

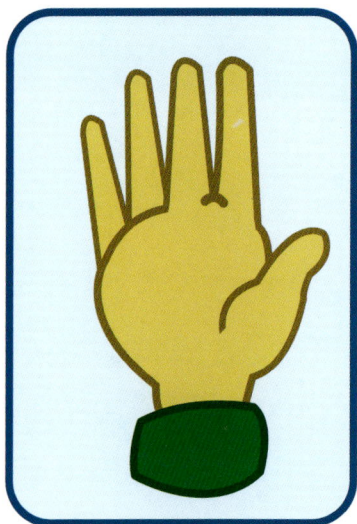

5

6

7

8

9

10

Acknowledgements

Some words in sign language have multiple acceptable signs. In those instances where multiple signs were available, Grandpa Don TM chose the sign most appropriate for Abby and Alyssa.

Grandpa Don TM encourages readers who want to learn more about sign language to read:

- "The Art of Sign Language" by
   Christopher Brown; Random House.

- "Webster's Unabridged American
   Sign Language Dictionary" by Elaine Costello, PHD.

And to also visit these websites:

- www.signingsavvy.com

- www.lessontutor.com